C000048646

MAJOR BOOKS OF JAMES JOYCE

Chamber Music (1907)

Dubliners (1914)

A Portrait of the Artist as a Young Man (1916)

Ulysses (1922)

Finnegans Wake (1939)

The Critical Writings (1959)

Stephen Hero (1969)

JAMES JOYCE

ON IBSEN

Edited with an Introduction
by Dennis Phillips

GREEN INTEGER
KØBENHAVN / LOS ANGELES
1999

GREEN INTEGER BOOKS
Edited by Per Bregne
København/Los Angeles

Distributed in the United States by Consortium Book
Sales and Distribution, 1045 Westgate Drive, Suite 90
Saint Paul, Minnesota 55114-1065
and in England and the Continent by
Central Books
99 Wallis Road, London E9 5LN
(323) 857-1115/http://www.sunmoon.com

First edition 1999
Introduction ©1999 by Dennis Phillips
Editorial selection ©1999 by Per Bregne
"Epilogue to Ibsen's Ghost," from *The Critical Writings
of James Joyce* by James Joyce, E. Mason and Richard Ellmann, editors
©1959 by Harriet Weaver and F. Lionel Monro, as Administrators
for the Estate of James Joyce, renewed ©1987 by F. Lionel Monro.
Used by permission of Viking Penguin, a division of Penguin Putnam, Inc.
All rights reserved.

Design: Per Bregne
Typography: Guy Bennett

LIBRARY OF CONGRESS CATALOGING IN PUBLICATION DATA
Joyce, James [1882–1941]
On Ibsen
ISBN: 1-55713-372-7
p. cm — Green Integer 12
I. Title II. Series

Contents

Introduction, by Dennis Phillips   7

Ibsen's New Drama   21

The Day of the Rabblement   65

Catilina   71

Epilogue to Ibsen's *Ghosts*   78

Ambition and Reverence: Joycean Juvenilia

THAT WE FIND interest in the juvenilia of James Joyce is not really surprising. In fact, as the necessity of dealing with the Gorman-Gilbert or Linati schemas on initial *Ulysses* assaults demonstrates, Joyce planned for his works to take place as much out of his texts as within them. Thus we read his early essays and declamations, not because they are inherently interesting, but because they are interesting *Joyceana*, adding links to a seemingly endless chain of clues to a collective riddle that is far from losing its allure.

Hugh Kenner, perhaps the most perceptive reader of *Ulysses*, has written that had Joyce stopped composing *Ulysses* after chapter ten, the world would have been left with an interesting, mildly unorthodox book, exhibiting little or nothing really innovative. Instead, of course, Joyce wrote another eight chapters, and, besides creating one of the landmark literary works of the century, created an academic industry of great vitality and apparently inexhaustible curiosity. That industry now is a part of the reading of *Ulysses*. When Joyce made his famous remark about keeping the professors guessing for a hundred years, it was the wily author of the whole, strategic *Ulysses* who exhibited his understanding of the components of one kind of immortality. He also underestimated the longevity of the industry he had begotten.

At the end of the century he helped to define, 116 years after his birth and fifty-seven years after his death, James Joyce passes the celebrity test of our current *fin de siècle*: all objects Joycean, all utterances Joycean, all juvenilia Joycean arrest the attention of the industry's captains and junior captains. Attributed to most other literary figures, including the nonexistent author of only the first ten chapters of *Ulysses*, the various by-products of the Joycean creative engine would merit far less study.

This is not to imply that much of the Joycean Trivia is not interesting. Kenner, notably, has taken the trivia of, for example, tram schedules, police statistics, and currency values, to illuminate the way *Ulysses* is read. Richard Ellmann brilliantly constructed a biography which blends a thorough and well-documented life history with valuable readings of Joyce's works. And, as an historical figure, James Joyce is one (certainly not the only) artistic character through whose work *and* life we come to expand our knowledge of the amazingly innovative and productive period that spans the beginning of the new century to the second World War.

It was on April 1, 1900, that Joyce's first "formal publication" appeared in the English *Fortnightly Review*. Joyce was 18 years old, and the article, "Ibsen's New Drama," was one of several pieces on Ibsen that the young Joyce would write. While still in college, and before he had begun even the preliminary stages of writing that would take him to *A Portrait of the Artist as a Young Man* and *Dubliners*, Joyce was making forays into the business of being a writer and becoming a *figure*.

Three of the four works printed in this volume ("Ibsen's New Drama," "The Day of the Rabblement," and "Catilina") represent, among many other Joycean things, the young writer's initial public steps in creating a place for himself in European (not Irish) Literature.

"Ibsen's New Drama" came into being as Joyce was preparing a paper called "Drama and Life," a defense of Ibsen, as well as a strong initial statement of personal poetics, which was to be delivered to the Literary and Historical Society of University College. Before delivering the paper, the 18 year-old received a reply to a letter of inquiry to W.L. Courtney, editor of the *Fortnightly Review*. Courtney's letter obliquely suggests that he could use a review of Ibsen's new play, "When We Dead Awaken." With this thin encouragement, Joyce submitted "Ibsen's New Drama," which was accepted by Courtney on January 3, 1900.

According to Stanilaus Joyce, publication in the *Fortnightly Review* distinguished Joyce among his classmates. This was certainly a pleasant victory. But even sweeter was a letter Joyce had received from William Archer, Ibsen's English translator:

> I think it will interest you to know that in a letter I had from Henrik Ibsen a day or two ago he says "I have read...a review by Mr James Joyce in the *Fortnightly Review* which is very benevolent...and for which I should like to

thank the author if only I had sufficient knowledge of the language."

For the formative Joyce, the naturalistic power of Ibsen's work and his unwavering pursuit of his ideas against a sometimes violent public disapproval were models of artistic conduct. Now the master had written to him. Joyce's reply to Archer is touching in its humility, all the more because it came at a time in Joyce's life when brash arrogance was one of his more blatant character traits:

> ...I am a young Irishman, eighteen years old, and the words of Ibsen I shall keep in my heart all my life.

For "Ibsen's New Drama," Joyce received the considerable sum of twelve guineas. Kenner points out that, in those days, it wasn't hard to scrape by on a pound a week. Here was enough money for Joyce's family to get by on for at least a month. Instead he took his dad to London. Many years hence, an older James Joyce would refer to himself as someone inclined toward extravagance, as the London trip might seem to evince. Extravagant maybe, but this trip was meant to build his career. During the night, Joyce and his father went to theater and music halls. During the days they kept appointments with various literary people, including Courtney and Archer.

There is no question that theater plays a large part in Joyce's work, particularly *Ulysses* and *Finnegans Wake*. Not only the obvious "interior monologue" (over which Joyce never claimed inventor status), but issues of structure, pacing, relationship to audience, questions of interiority versus exteriority, to name a few characteristics which can be identified with Joyce's work, have a profound root in the literature and traditions of the theater. It was fitting and useful for the Joyces to visit the vital world of the London stage.

There is also no question that from an early point in Joyce's development, he realized that fame, serious, long-lasting, but also immediate and popular fame, required a great deal of attention, not to mention positioning and strategy. It was, therefore, logical that Joyce used most of the twelve guineas (he left a pound with his mother) to fortify the two important contacts which "Ibsen's New Drama" had yielded. That he was reaching across the channel to the English literary establishment, that he was writing on a Norwegian dramatist, are crucial to the position he was seeking to take. He reinvested his first royalty payment to help further his hope for a life-long career.

Among the aspects of Joyce's genius was his acute sense of where in history he was, and how to utilize that knowledge to his best advantage. In fact, that particular form of self-consciousness, and a willingness and an ability to act upon it, is something prominently Modernist. Among his peers, Joyce was not alone in understanding the very worldly nature of how literary canonization is achieved.

In March 1901, almost a year after Archer communicated Ibsen's thanks, Joyce, on the occasion of Ibsen's 73rd birthday, wrote a letter of "greeting." As Ellmann says, "This was the sort of letter that the recipient discards hastily and the writer files away." What Ibsen did with the letter may be known to a functionary in the Ibsen Industry. Joyce kept a copy for his own future industry, and left a record of a young writer paying his respects to an eminent elder, and a very confidant, ambitious and self-appointed successor announcing his place on the short list of passed-torch recipients.

…I have sounded your name defiantly through the college where it was either unknown or known faintly and darkly. I have claimed for you your rightful place in the history of the drama. I have shown what, as it seemed to me, was your highest excellence—your lofty impersonal power…. But we always keep the dearest things to ourselves. I did not tell them what bound me closest to you. I did not say how what I could discern dimly of your life was my pride to see, how your battles inspired me—not the obvious material battles but those that were fought and won behind your forehead, how your wilful resolution to wrest the secret from life gave me heart and how in your absolute indifference to public canons of art, friends and shibboleths you walked in the light of your inward heroism…. Your work on earth draws to a close and you are near the silence.

It is growing dark for you. Many write of such things, but they do not know. You have only opened the way—though you have gone as far as you could upon it.... But I am sure that higher and holier enlightenment lies—onward.[1]

While Joyce was "sounding [Ibsen's] name defiantly through" University College, William Butler Yeats, et al, were seeking a different kind of theatrical realization. Yeats, or so Joyce thought, was pandering to the Irish masses. To the increasingly Europeanized Joyce, this was an artistic betrayal. While Ibsen seemed to be warring with the "trolls," as Ellmann observes, Yeats seemed to be catering to what Joyce called "the most belated race in Europe."

On October 14, 1901 Joyce wrote "The Day of the Rabblement," professing his view of the artist's isolation from the whims and tastes of hoi polloi. As an insight into Joyce's mature work, particularly the

---

1 *James Joyce Letters*, volume one, page 51, Stuart Gilbert, editor, The Viking Press, 1966.

complex politics (some think lack of politics) that ac-
company the making of work as vulnerable to a charge
of "elitism" as *Ulysses* and *Finnegans Wake* are, this
essay has a more traditional "literary" value than the
directly Ibsen-related pieces do. But Ibsen is not ab-
sent from "The Day of the Rabblement." He is
Joyce's model, his portrait of the mature artist, filled
with "inner approbation" (as Joyce once described
his own process), pursuing his work without yield-
ing to the external pressures to be "understood" or
"accepted."

The eighteen months that elapsed between the
publications of "The Day of the Rabblement" and
his review of Ibsen's first play, "Catilina," find Joyce
attempting to establish himself as a critic, a job which
would serve the duel role of revenue and reputation
building. His valuable four month sojourn in Paris,
referenced in *A Portrait of the Artist as a Young Man*
and *Ulysses*, occurred at this time. (He left Dublin
for Paris on December 1, 1902.)

Among the important factors of this period is the
fact that, despite Joyce's flamboyant opposition to
some of the established Irish literary figures, he was

able to summon the support of the most prominent of them, including, remarkably, Yeats.

Joyce perused his connection with William Archer, but after Archer's appreciative but critical responses to a play and a group of poems, the correspondence stops.

At the same time, Joyce had managed to interest the poet George Russell enough to allow Russell the chance to see the tremendous talent emerging from Joyce. Russell then connected Joyce with Yeats, among others, and Yeats, generously unconcerned with Joyce's qualified condemnation of him as having a "floating will" and a "treacherous instinct," was helpful to Joyce in establishing his toehold as a critic, especially with the *Speaker*.

On March 21, 1903, while in Paris, through the Yeats connection, Joyce reviewed for the *Speaker* the French translation of Ibsen's 1848 play, "Catilina." In the review he reaffirms his theme of the solitary artist, indifferent "to public canons of art, friends and shibboleths." Stanilaus Joyce observes in *My Brother's Keeper*, "When he points out the unflinching courage with which Ibsen pursued his purpose so calmly and ironically...the words are almost prophetical of my brother's own struggle and triumph that were to come."

At this point Joyce had written little more than a few poems, a couple of abandoned plays and a handful of reviews. By positioning himself outside the various literary circles, Joyce was free to interact with the figures of the circles without becoming anyone's acolyte. His resolute independence contributed to a mystique which supported, perhaps created, the interest others had in him. Joyce knew that a portion of the fate of his incipient industry would depend on that type of interest.

In 1934, the 52-year-old Joyce, 12 years into the 17-year labor on *Finnegans Wake*, and internationally famous as the author of *Ulysses* (the Woolsey opinion that lifted the U.S. ban was made in December of 1933), composed the coda to his earlier writings on Ibsen. It came in the form of a satirical poem meant to be an epilogue to "Ghosts." According to Ellmann, Joyce was concerned that the poem would be read as autobiographical. He was careful to tell his official record keeper, Stuart Gilbert, to attribute the work to an earlier period on the Joyce time line. At this point in his life, Joyce had achieved a level of recognition that has more or less held steady since. But after his irreverent treatment of his master's play, Joyce was anxious to direct future readings of this minor piece. As Ellmann records, Joyce spun a bit of revisionism for Gilbert to place in his biography:

> This (which is in fact a grotesque amplification of Osvalt's own attempted defense of his father in the play) is not to be interpreted, however, in the sense that he [Joyce] does not consider Ibsen to be the supreme dramatic poet, basing his belief, however, on the plays from the *Wild Duck* onwards, and of course does not mean that he considers *Ghosts* as anything but a great tragedy.

With the distance of 31 years and the achievement of his own mastery, Joyce was struck by aspects of Ibsen's work which he thought were worthy of criticism. His loyalty to Ibsen, however, and the place Joyce maintained for him in his personal canon, was not something Joyce wanted misinterpreted. At this point in his life he had no doubt that anything he wrote would become material for the industry he had begun creating while still in college.

Joyce's remark about "inner approbation" is contained in a letter to his father, displayed in a glass case in the Joyce Museum which is in the Martello Tower in Sandymount (outside of Dublin), that Joyce had once lived in and in which he set the opening of *Ulysses*. He wrote the letter as the first discouraging comments about *Finnegans Wake* were coming to him. Whatever Joyce's strategies were to ensure literary immortality, at the beginning and end of his career he faced dismissal, disapproval, scorn, even ridicule. He must have taken a lesson and some comfort from Ibsen's having previously overcome similar difficulties while continuing to produce work which Joyce held in the highest regard. The documentary trail he left behind enriches our fulfillment of his enormous project.

—DENNIS PHILLIPS
June 1998

Ibsen's New Drama

TWENTY YEARS have passed since Henrik Ibsen wrote *A Doll's House*, thereby almost marking an epoch in the history of drama. During those years his name has gone abroad through the length and breath of two continents, and has provoked more discussion and criticism than that of any other living man. He has been upheld as a religious reformer, a social reformer, a Semitic lover of righteousness, and as a great dramatist. He has been rigorously denounced as a meddlesome intruder, a defective artist, an incomprehensible mystic, and, in the eloquent words of a certain English critic, "a muck-ferreting dog." Through the perplexities of such diverse criticism, the great genius of the man is day by day coming out as a hero comes out amid the earthly trials. The dissonant cries are fainter and more distant, the random praises are rising in steadier and more choral chaunt. Even to the uninterested bystander it must seem significant that the interest attached to this

Norwegian has never flagged for over a quarter of a century. It may be questioned whether any man has held so firm an empire over the thinking world in modern times. Not Rousseau; not Emerson; not Carlyle; not any of those giants of whom almost all have passed out of human ken. Ibsen's power over two generations has been enhanced by his own reticence. Seldom, if at all, has he condescended to join battle with his enemies. It would appear as if the storm of fierce debate rarely broke in upon his wonderful calm. The conflicting voices have not influenced his work in the very smallest degree. His output of dramas has been regulated by the utmost order, by a clockwork routine, seldom found in the case of genius. Only once he answered his assailants after their violent attack on *Ghosts*. But from *The Wild Duck* to *John Gabriel Borkman,* his dramas have appeared almost mechanically at intervals of two years. One is apt to overlook the sustained energy which such a plan of campaign demands; but even surprise at this must give way to admiration at the gradual, irresistible advance of this extraordinary man. Eleven plays, all dealing with modern life, have been published. Here is the list: *A Doll's House, Ghosts, An Enemy of the People, The Wild Duck, Rosmersholm, The Lady from the Sea, Hedda Gabler, The Master Builder, Little Eyolf, John Gabriel Borkman,* and lastly—his new drama, published at Copenhagen, December 19th, 1899—*When We Dead Awaken.* This play is already in process of translation into almost a dozen different languages—a fact which speaks volumes for the power of its author. The drama is written in prose, and is in three acts.

To begin an account of a play of Ibsen's is surely no easy matter. The subject is, in one way, so confined, and, in another way, so vast. It is safe to predict that nine-tenths of the notices of this play will open in some such way as the following: "Arnold Rubek and his wife, Maja, have been married for four years, at the beginning of the play. Their union is, however, unhappy. Each is discontented with the other." So far as this goes, it is unimpeachable; but then it does not go very far. It does not convey even the most shadowy notion of the relations between Professor Rubek and his wife. It is a bald, clerkly version of countless, indefinable complexities. It is as though the history of a tragic life were to be written down rudely in two columns, one for the pros and the other for the cons. It is only saying what is literally true, to say that, in the three acts of the drama, there has been stated all that is essential to the drama. There is from first to last hardly a superfluous word or phrase. Therefore, the play itself expresses its own ideas as briefly and as concisely as they can be expressed in the dramatic form. It is manifest, then, that a notice cannot give an adequate notion of the drama. This is not the case with the common lot of plays, to which the fullest justice may be meted out in a very limited number of lines. They are for the most part reheated dishes—unoriginal compositions, cheerfully owlish as to heroic insight, living only in their own candid claptrap—in a word, stagey. The most perfunctory curtness is their fittest meed. But in dealing with the work of a man like Ibsen, the task set the reviewer is truly great enough to sink all his courage. All he can hope to do is to link some of the more salient points together in such a way as to suggest rather than to indicate, the intricacies of the plot. Ibsen has attained ere this to such mastery over his art that, with apparently easy dialogue, he presents his men and women passing through different soul-crises. His analytic method is thus made use of to the fullest extent, and into the comparatively short space of two days the life in life of all his characters is compressed. For instance, though we only see Solness during one night and up to the following evening, we have in reality watched with bated breath the whole course of his life up to the moment when Hilda Wangel enters his house. So in the play under consideration, when we see Professor Rubek first, he is sitting in a garden chair, reading his morning paper, but by degrees the whole scroll of his life is unrolled before us, and we have the pleasure not of hearing it read out to us, but of reading it for ourselves, piecing the various parts, and going closer to see wherever the writing on the parchment is fainter or less legible.

As I have said, when the play opens, Professor Rubek is sitting in the gardens of a hotel, eating, or rather having finished, his breakfast. In another chair, close beside him, is sitting Maja Rubek, the Professor's wife. The scene is in Norway, a popular health resort near the sea. Through the trees can be seen the town harbor, and the fjord, with steamers plying over it, as it stretches past headland and river-isle out to the sea. Rubek is a famous sculptor, of middle age, and Maja, a woman still young, whose bright eyes have just a shade of sadness in them. These two continue reading their respective papers quietly in the peace of the morning. All looks so idyllic to the careless eye. The lady breaks the silence in a weary, petulant manner by complaining of the deep peace that reigns about them. Arnold lays down his paper with mild expostulation. Then they begin to converse of this thing and that; first of the silence, then of the place and the people, of the railway stations through which they passed the previous night, with their sleepy porters and aimlessly shifting lanterns. From this they proceed to talk of the changes in the people, and of all that has grown up since they were married. Then it is but a little further to the main trouble. In speaking of their married life it speedily appears that the inner view of their relations is hardly as ideal as the outward view might lead one to expect. The depths of these two people are being slowly stirred up. The leaven of prospective drama is gradually discerned working amid the *fin-de-siècle* scene. The lady seems a difficult little person. She complains of the idle promises with which her husband had fed her aspirations.

MAJA. You said you would take me up to a high mountain and show me all the glory of the world.

RUBEK (*with a slight start*). Did I promise you that, too?

In short, there is something untrue lying at the root of their union. Meanwhile the guests of the hotel, who are taking the baths, pass out of the hotel porch on the right, chatting and laughing men and women. They are informally marshaled by the inspector of the baths. This person is an unmistakable type of the conventional official. He salutes Mr. and Mrs. Rubek, inquiring how they slept. Rubek asks him if any of the guests take their baths by night, as he has seen a white figure moving in the park during the night. Maja scouts the notion, but the inspector says that there is a strange lady who has rented the pavilion which is to the left, and who is staying there, with one attendant—a Sister of Mercy. As they are talking, the strange lady and her companion pass slowly through the park and enter the pavilion. The incident appears to affect Rubek, and Maja's curiosity is aroused.

MAJA (*a little hurt and jarred*). Perhaps this lady has been one of your models, Rubek? Search your memory.

RUBEK (*looks cuttingly at her*). Model?

MAJA (*with a provoking smile*). In your younger days, I mean. You are said to have had such innumerable models—long ago, of course.

RUBEK (*in the same tone*). Oh, no, little Frau Maja. I have in reality had only one single model. One and one only for everything I have done.

While this misunderstanding is finding outlet in the foregoing conversation, the inspector, all at once, takes fright at some person who is approaching. He attempts to escape into the hotel, but the high-pitched voice of the person who is approaching arrests him.

ULFHEIM'S voice (*heard outside*). Stop a moment, man. Devil take it all, can't you stop? Why do you always scuttle away from me?

With these words, uttered in strident tones, the second chief actor enters on the scene. He is described as a great bear-killer, thin, tall, of uncertain age, and muscular. He is accompanied by his servant, Lars, and a couple of sporting dogs. Lars does not speak a single word in the play. Ulfheim at present dismisses him with a kick, and approaches Mr. and Mrs. Rubek. He falls into conversation with them, for Rubek is known to him as the celebrated sculptor. On sculpture this savage hunter offers some original remarks.

ULFHEIM ... We both work in a hard material, madam—both your husband and I. He struggles with his marble blocks, I daresay;

29

and I struggle with tense and quivering
bear-sinews. And we both of us win the fight
in the end—subdue and master our material. We don't give in until we have got the
better of it, though it fight never so hard.

RUBEK (*deep in thought*). There's a great deal
of truth in what you say.

This eccentric creature, perhaps by the force of
his own eccentricity, has begun to weave a spell of
enchantment about Maja. Each word that he utters
tends to wrap the web of his personality still closer
about her. The black dress of the Sister of Mercy
causes him to grin sardonically. He speaks calmly of
all his near friends, whom he has dispatched out of
the world.

MAJA. And what did you do for your nearest
friends?

ULFHEIM. Shot them, of course.

RUBEK (*looking at him*). Shot them?

MAJA (*moving her chair back*). Shot them dead?

ULFHEIM (*nods*). I never miss, madam.

However, it turns out that by his nearest friends he means his dogs, and the minds of his hearers are put somewhat more at ease. During their conversation the Sister of Mercy has prepared a slight repast for her mistress at one of the tables outside the pavilion. The unsustaining qualities of the food excite Ulfheim's merriment. He speaks with a lofty disparagement of such effeminate diet. He is a realist in his appetite.

> ULFHEIM (*rising*). Spoken like a woman of spirit, madam. Come with me, then! They [his dogs] swallow whole, great, thumping meat-bones—gulp them up and then gulp them down again. Oh, it's a regular treat to see them!

On such half-gruesome, half-comic invitation Maja goes out with him, leaving her husband in the company of the strange lady who enters from the pavilion. Almost simultaneously the Professor and the lady recognize each other. The lady has served

Rubek as model for the central figure in his famous masterpiece, "The Resurrection Day." Having done her work for him, she had fled in an unaccountable manner, leaving no traces behind her. Rubek and she drift into familiar conversation. She asks him who is the lady who has just gone out. He answers, with some hesitation, that she is his wife. Then he asks if she is married. She replies that she is married. He asks her where her husband is at present.

RUBEK. And where is he now?

IRENE. Oh, in a churchyard somewhere or other, with a fine, handsome monument over him; and with a bullet rattling in his skull.

RUBEK. Did he kill himself?

IRENE. Yes, he was good enough to take that off my hands.

RUBEK. Do you not lament his loss, Irene?

IRENE. (*not understanding*). Lament? What loss?

RUBEK. Why, the loss of Herr von Satow, of course.

IRENE. His name was not Satow.

RUBEK. Was it not?

IRENE. My second husband is called Satow. He is a Russian.

RUBEK. And where is he?

IRENE. Far away in the Ural Mountains. Among all his goldmines.

RUBEK. So he lives there?

IRENE. (*shrugs her shoulders*). Lives? Lives? In reality I have killed him.

RUBEK. (*starts*). Killed— !

IRENE. Killed him with a fine sharp dagger which I always have with me in bed—

Rubek begins to understand that there is some meaning hidden beneath these strange words. He begins to think seriously on himself, his art, and on her, passing in review the course of his life since the creation of his masterpiece, "The Resurrection Day." He sees that he has not fulfilled the promise of that work, and comes to realize that there is something lacking in his life. He asks Irene how she has lived since they last saw each other. Irene's answer to his query is of great importance, for it strikes the key note of the entire play.

> IRENE (*rises slowly from her chair and says quiveringly*). I was dead for many years. They came and bound me—lacing my arms together at my back. Then they lowered me into a grave-vault, with iron bars before the loophole. And with padded walls, so that no one on the earth above could hear the grave-shrieks.

In Irene's allusion to her position as model for the great picture, Ibsen gives further proof of his extraordinary knowledge of women. No other man could have so subtly expressed the nature of the relations between the sculptor and his model, had he even dreamt of them.

> IRENE. I exposed myself wholly and unreservedly to your gaze [*more softly*] and never once did you touch me....
>
> ...

RUBEK (*looks impressively at her*). I was an artist, Irene.
IRENE (*darkly*). That is just it. That is just it.

Thinking deeper and deeper on himself and on
his former attitude towards this woman, it strikes him
yet more forcibly that there are great gulfs set between
his art and his life, and that even in his art his skill
and genius are far from perfect. Since Irene left him
he has done nothing but paint portrait busts of
townsfolk. Finally, some kind of resolution is en-
kindled in him, a resolution to repair his botching,
for he does not altogether despair of that. There is
just a reminder of the will-glorification of *Brand* in
the lines that follow.

RUBEK (*struggling with himself, uncertainly*).
If we could, oh, if only we could ....
IRENE. Why can we not do what we will?

In fine, the two agree in deeming their present
state insufferable. It appears plain to her that Rubek
lies under a heavy obligation to her, and with their

recognition of this, and the entrance of Maja, fresh from the enchantment of Ulfheim, the first act closes.

RUBEK. When did you begin to seek for me, Irene?

IRENE (*with a touch of jesting bitterness*). From the time when I realized that I had given away to you something rather indispensable. Something one ought never to part with.

RUBEK (*bowing his head*). Yes, that is bitterly true. You gave me three or four years of your youth.

IRENE. More, more than that I gave you— spendthrift as I then was.

RUBEK. Yes, you were prodigal, Irene. You gave me all your naked loveliness—

IRENE. To gaze upon—

RUBEK. And to glorify . . . .

   …

IRENE. But you have forgotten the most precious gift.

RUBEK. The most precious . . . what gift was that?

IRENE. I gave you my young living soul. And that gift left me empty within—soulless [*looks at him with a fixed stare*]. It was that I died of, Arnold.

It is evident, even from this mutilated account, that the first act is a masterly one. With no perceptible effort the drama rises, with a methodic natural ease it develops. The trim garden of the nineteenth-century hotel is slowly made the scene of a gradually growing dramatic struggle. Interest has been roused in each of the characters, sufficient to carry the mind into the succeeding act. The situation is not stupidly explained, but the action has set in, and at the close the play has reached a definite stage of progression.

The second act takes place close to a sanatorium on the mountains. A cascade leaps from a rock and flows in steady stream to the right. On the bank some children are playing, laughing and shouting. The time is evening. Rubek is discovered lying on a mound to the left. Maja enters shortly, equipped for hill-climbing. Helping herself with her stick across the stream, she calls out to Rubek and approaches him. He asks how she and her companion are amusing themselves, and questions her as to their hunting. An exquisitely humorous touch enlivens their talk. Rubek asks if they intend hunting the bear near the surrounding locality. She replies with a grand superiority.

MAJA. You don't suppose that bears are to be found in the naked mountains, do you?

The next topic is the uncouth Ulfheim. Maja admires him because he is so ugly—then turns abruptly to her husband saying, pensively, that he also is ugly. The accused pleads his age.

RUBEK (*shrugging his shoulders*). One grows old. One grows old, Frau Maja!

This semi-serious banter leads them on to graver matters. Maja lies at length in the soft heather, and rails gently at the Professor. For the mysteries and claims of art she has a somewhat comical disregard.

MAJA (*with a somewhat scornful laugh*). Yes, you are always, always an artist.

and again—

MAJA. ... Your tendency is to keep yourself to yourself and—think your own thoughts. And, of course, I can't talk properly to you about your affairs. I know nothing about Art and that sort of thing. [*With an impatient gesture.*] And care very little either, for that matter.

She rallies him on the subject of the strange lady, and hints maliciously at the understanding between them. Rubek says that he was only an artist and that she was the source of his inspiration. He confesses that the five years of his married life have been years of intellectual famine for him. He has viewed in their true light his own feelings towards his art.

RUBEK (*smiling*). But that was not precisely what I had in my mind.

MAJA. What then?

RUBEK (*again serious*). It was this—that all the talk about the artist's vocation and the artist's mission, and so forth, began to strike me as being very empty and hollow and meaningless at bottom.

MAJA. Then what would you put in its place?

RUBEK. Life, Maja.

The all-important question of their mutual happiness is touched upon, and after a brisk discussion a tacit agreement to separate is effected. When matters are in this happy condition Irene is descried coming across the heath. She is surrounded by the sportive children and stays awhile among them. Maja jumps up from the grass and goes to her, saying, enigmatically, that her husband requires assistance to "open a precious casket." Irene bows and goes towards Rubek, and Maja goes joyfully to seek her hunter. The interview which follows is certainly remarkable, even from a stagey point of view. It constitutes, practically, the substance of the second act, and is of absorbing interest. At the same time it must be added that such a scene would tax the powers of the mimes producing it. Nothing short of a complete realization of the two *rôles* would represent the complex ideas involved in the conversation. When we reflect how few stage artists would have either the intelligence to attempt it or the powers to execute it, we behold a pitiful revelation.

In the interview of these two people on the heath, the whole tenors of their lives are outlined with bold steady strokes. From the first exchange of introductory words each phrase tells a chapter of experiences. Irene alludes to the dark shadow of the Sister of Mercy which follows her everywhere, as the shadow of Arnold's unquiet conscience follows him. When he has half-involuntarily confessed so much, one of the great barriers between them is broken down. Their trust in each other is, to some extent, renewed, and they revert to their past acquaintance. Irene speaks openly of her feelings, of her hate for the sculptor.

IRENE (*again vehemently*). Yes, for you—for the artist who had so lightly and carelessly taken a warm-blooded body, a young human life, and worn the soul out of it—because you needed it for a work of art.

Rubek's transgression has indeed been great. Not merely has he possessed himself of her soul, but he has withheld from its rightful throne the child of her soul. By her child Irene means the statue. To her it seems that this statue is, in a very true and very real sense, born of her. Each day as she saw it grow to its full growth under the hand of the skilful molder, her inner sense of motherhood for it, of right over it, of love towards it, had become stronger and more confirmed.

IRENE (*changing to a tone full of warmth and feeling*). But that statue in the wet, living clay, that I loved—as it rose up, a vital human creature out of these raw, shapeless masses —for that was our creation, our child. Mine and yours.

It is, in reality, because of her strong feelings that

she has kept aloof from Rubek for five years. But when she hears now of what he has done to the child—her child—all her powerful nature rises up against him in resentment. Rubek, in a mental agony, endeavors to explain, while she listens like a tigress whose cub has been wrested from her by a thief.

> RUBEK. I was young then—with no experience of life. The Resurrection, I thought, would be most beautifully and exquisitely figured as a young unsullied woman—with none of a life's experience—awakening to light and glory without having to put away from her anything ugly and impure.

With larger experience of life he has found it necessary to alter his ideal somewhat, he has made her child no longer a principal, but an intermediary figure. Rubek, turning towards her, sees her just about to stab him. In a fever of terror and thought he rushes into his own defense, pleading madly for the errors he has done. It seems to Irene that he is endeavoring to render his sin poetical, that he is penitent but in a luxury of dolor. The thought that she has given up herself, her whole life, at the bidding of his false art, rankles in her heart with a terrible persistence. She cries out against herself, not loudly, but in deep sorrow.

IRENE (*With apparent self-control*). I should have borne children into the world—many children—real children—not such children as are hidden away in grave-vaults. That was my vocation. I ought never to have served you—poet.

Rubek, in poetic absorption, has no reply, he is musing on the old, happy days. Their dead joys solace him. But Irene is thinking of a certain phrase of his which he had spoken unwittingly. He had declared that he owed her thanks for her assistance in his work. This has been, he had said, a truly blessed *episode* in my life. Rubek's tortured mind cannot bear any more reproaches, too many are heaped upon it already. He begins throwing flowers on the stream, as they used in those bygone days on the lake of

Taunitz. He recalls to her the time when they made a boat of leaves, and yoked a white swan to it, in imitation of the boat of Lohengrin. Even here in their sport there lies a hidden meaning.

> IRENE. You said I was the swan that drew your
> boat.
> RUBEK. Did I say so? Yes, I daresay I did [*absorbed in the game*]. Just see how the sea-gulls are swimming down the stream!
> IRENE (*laughing*). And all your ships have run ashore.
> RUBEK (*throwing more leaves into the brook*). I have ships enough in reserve.

While they are playing aimlessly, in a kind of childish despair, Ulfheim and Maja appear across the heath. These two are going to seek adventures on the high tablelands. Maja sings out to her husband a little song which she has composed in her joyful mood. With a sardonic laugh Ulfheim bids Rubek good- night and disappears with his companion up the mountain. All at once Irene and Rubek leap to the same thought. But at that moment the gloomy figure of the Sister of Mercy is seen in the twilight, with her leaden eyes looking at them both. Irene breaks from him, but promises to meet him that night on the heath.

RUBEK. And you will come, Irene?

IRENE. Yes, certainly I will come. Wait for me here.

RUBEK (*repeats dreamily*). Summer night on the upland. With you. With you. [*His eyes meet hers.*] Oh, Irene, that might have been our life. And that we have forfeited, we two.

IRENE. We see the irretrievable only when [*breaks short off*].

RUBEK (*looks inquiringly at her*). When? . . .

IRENE. When we dead awaken.

The third act takes place on a wide plateau, high up on the hills. The ground is rent with yawning clefts. Looking to the right, one sees the range of the summits half-hidden in the moving mists. On the left stands an old, dismantled hut. It is in the early morning, when the skies are the color of pearl. The day is beginning to break. Maja and Ulfheim come down to the plateau. Their feelings are sufficiently explained by the opening words.

> MAJA (*trying to tear herself loose*). Let me go! Let me go, I say!
> ULFHEIM. Come, come! are you going to bite now? You're as snappish as a wolf.

When Ulfheim will not cease his annoyances, Maja threatens to run over the crest of the neighboring ridge. Ulfheim points out that she will dash herself to pieces. He has wisely sent Lars away after the hounds, that he may be uninterrupted. Lars, he says, may be trusted not to find the dogs too soon.

> MAJA (*looking angrily at him*). No, I daresay not.
> ULFHEIM (*catching at her arm*). For Lars—he knows my—methods of sport, you see.

Maja, with enforced self-possession, tells him frankly what she thinks of him. Her uncomplimentary observations please the bear-hunter very much. Maja requires all her tact to keep him in order. When she talks of going back to the hotel, he gallantly offers to carry her on his shoulders, for which suggestion he is promptly snubbed. The two are playing as a cat and a bird play. Out of their skirmish one speech of Ulfheim's rises suddenly to arrest attention, as it throws some light on his former life.

ULFHEIM (*with suppressed exasperation*). I once took a young girl—lifted her up from the mire of the streets, and carried her in my arms. Next my heart I carried her. So I would have borne her all through life, lest haply she should dash her foot against a stone .... [*with a growling laugh.*] And do you know what I got for my reward?

MAJA. No. What did you get?

ULFHEIM. (*looks at her, smiles and nods*). I got the horns! The horns that you can see so plainly. Is not that a comical story, madam bear-murderess?

As an exchange of confidence, Maja tells him her life in summary—and chiefly her married life with Professor Rubek. As a result, these two uncertain souls feel attracted to each other, and Ulfheim states his case in the following characteristic manner:

ULFHEIM. Should not we two tack our poor
　　shreds of life together?

Maja, satisfied that in their vows there will be no promise on his part to show her all the splendors of the earth, or to fill her dwelling-place with art, gives a half-consent by allowing him to carry her down the slope. As they are about to go, Rubek and Irene, who have also spent the night on the heath, approach the same plateau. When Ulfheim asks Rubek if he and Madame have ascended by the same pathway, Rubek answers significantly.

RUBEK. Yes, of course [*with a glance at* MAJA].
　　Henceforth the strange lady and I do not
　　intend our ways to part.

While the musketry of their wit is at work, the elements seem to feel that there is a mighty problem to be solved then and there, and that a great drama is swiftly drawing to a close. The smaller figures of Maja and Ulfheim are grown still smaller in the dawn of the tempest. Their lots are decided in comparative quiet, and we cease to take much interest in them. But the other two hold our gaze, as they stand up silently on the fjaell, engrossing central figures of boundless, human interest. On a sudden, Ulfheim raises his hand impressively towards the heights.

ULFHEIM. But don't you see that the storm is upon us? Don't you hear the blasts of wind?

RUBEK (*listening*). They sound like the prelude to the Resurrection Day.

...

MAJA (*drawing* ULFHEIM *away*). Let us make haste and get down.

As he cannot take more than one person at a time, Ulfheim promises to send aid for Rubek and Irene, and, seizing Maja in his arms, clambers rapidly but warily down the path. On the desolate mountain plateau, in the growing light, the man and the woman are left together—no longer the artist and his model. And the shadow of a great change is stalking close in the morning silence. Then Irene tells Arnold that she will not go back among the men and women she has left; she will not be rescued. She tells him also, for now she may tell all, how she had been tempted to kill him in frenzy when he spoke of their connection as an episode of his life.

RUBEK (*darkly*). And why did you hold your hand?

IRENE. Because it flashed upon me with a sudden horror that you were dead already—long ago.

But, says Rubek, our love is not dead in us, it is active, fervent and strong.

IRENE. The love that belongs to the life of earth—the beautiful, miraculous life of earth—the inscrutable life of earth—that is dead in both of us.

There are, moreover, the difficulties of their former lives. Even here, at the sublimest part of his play, Ibsen is master of himself and his facts. His genius as an artist faces all, shirks nothing. At the close of *The Master Builder,* the greatest touch of all was the horrifying exclamation of one without, "O! the head is all crushed in." A lesser artist would have cast a spiritual glamour over the tragedy of Bygmester Solness. In like manner here Irene objects that she has exposed herself as a nude before the vulgar gaze, that Society has cast her out, that all is too late. But Rubek cares for such considerations no more. He flings them all to the wind and decides.

RUBEK (*throwing his arms violently around her*). Then let two of the dead—us two—for once live life to its uttermost, before we go down to our graves again.

IRENE (*with a shriek*). Arnold!

RUBEK. But not here in the half-darkness. Not here with this hideous dank shroud flapping around us!

IRENE (*carried away by passion*). No, no—up

in the light and in all the glittering glory!
Up to the Peak of Promise!

RUBEK. There we will hold our marriage-feast,
Irene—oh! my beloved!

IRENE (*proudly*). The sun may freely look on
us, Arnold.

RUBEK. All the powers of light may freely look
on us—and all the powers of darkness too
[*seizes her hand*]— if you then follow me,
oh my grace-given bride!

IRENE (*as though transfigured*). I follow you,
freely and gladly, my lord and master!

RUBEK (*drawing her along with him*). We
must first pass through the mists, Irene, and
then—

IRENE. Yes, through all the mists, and then
right up to the summit of the tower that
shines in the sunrise.

The mist-clouds close in over the scene.
RUBEK *and* IRENE, *hand in hand, climb up
over the snowfield to the right and soon dis-
appear among the lower clouds. Keen storm-
gusts hurtle and whistle through the air.*

The SISTER OF MERCY *appears upon the rubble-slope to the left. She stops and looks around silently and searchingly.*

MAJA *can be heard singing triumphantly far in the depths below.*

MAJA. I am free! I am free! I am free! No more life in the prison for me! I am free as a bird! I am free!

Suddenly a sound like thunder is heard from high up on the snowfield, which glides and whirls downwards with rushing speed. RUBEK *and* IRENE *can be dimly discerned as they are whirled along with the masses of snow and buried in them.*

THE SISTER OF MERCY (*gives a shriek, stretches out her arms towards them, and cries*), Irene! [*Stands silent a moment, then makes the sign of the cross before her in the air, and says*], Pax Vobiscum!

MAJA'S *triumphant song sounds from still further down below.*

Such is the plot, in a crude and incoherent way, of this new drama. Ibsen's plays do not depend for their interest on the action, or on the incidents. Even the characters, faultlessly drawn though they be, are not the first thing in his plays. But the naked drama— either the perception of a great truth, or the opening up of a great question, or a great conflict which is almost independent of the conflicting actors, and has been and is of far-reaching importance—this is what primarily rivets our attention. Ibsen has chosen the average lives in their uncompromising truth for the groundwork of all his later plays. He has abandoned the verse form, and has never sought to embellish his work after the conventional fashion. Even as his dramatic theme reached its zenith he has not sought to trick it out in gawds or tawdriness. How easy it would have been to have written *An Enemy of the People* on a speciously loftier level—to have replaced the *bourgeois* by the legitimate hero! Critics might then have extolled as grand what they have so often condemned as banal. But the surroundings are nothing to Ibsen. The play is the thing. By the force of his genius, and the indisputable skill which he brings to all his efforts, Ibsen has, for many years, engrossed the attention of the civilized world. Many years more, however, must pass before he will enter his kingdom in jubilation, although, as he stands today, all has been done on his part to ensure his own worthiness to enter therein. I do not propose here to examine into every detail of dramaturgy connected with this play, but merely to outline the characterization.

In his characters Ibsen does not repeat himself. In this drama—the last of a long catalogue—he has drawn and differentiated with his customary skill. What a novel creation is Ulfheim! Surely the hand which has drawn him has not yet lost her cunning. Ulfheim is, I think, the newest character in the play. He is a kind of surprise-packet. It is as a result of his novelty that he seems to leap, at first mention, into bodily form. He is superbly wild, primitively impressive. His fierce eyes roll and glare as those of Yégof or Herne. As for Lars, we may dismiss him, for he never opens his mouth. The Sister of Mercy speaks only once in the play, but then with good effect. In silence she follows Irene like a retribution, a voiceless shadow with her own symbolic majesty.

Irene, too, is worthy of her place in the gallery of her compeers. Ibsen's knowledge of humanity is nowhere more obvious than in his portrayal of women. He amazes one by his painful introspection; he seems to know them better than they know themselves. Indeed, if one may say so of an eminently virile man, there is a curious admixture of the woman in his nature. His marvelous accuracy, his faint traces of femininity, his delicacy of swift touch, are perhaps attributed to this admixture. But that he knows women is an incontrovertible fact. He appears to have sounded them to almost unfathomable depths. Beside his portraits the psychological studies of Hardy and Turgénieff, or the exhaustive elaborations of Meredith, seem no more than sciolism. With a deft stroke, in a phrase, in a word, he does what costs them chapters, and does it better. Irene, then, has to face great comparison; but it must be acknowledged that she comes forth of it bravely. Although Ibsen's women are uniformly true, they, of course, present themselves in various lights. Thus Gina Ekdal is, before all else, a comic figure, and Hedda Gabler a tragic one—if such old-world terms may be employed without incongruity. But Irene cannot be so readily classified; the very aloofness from passion, which is not separable from her, forbids classification. She interests us strangely—magnetically, because of her inner power of character. However perfect Ibsen's former creations may be, it is questionable whether any of his women reach to the depth of soul of Irene. She holds our gaze for the sheer force of her intellectual capacity. She is, moreover, an intensely spiritual creation—in the truest and widest sense of that. At times she is liable to get beyond us, to soar above us, as she does with Rubek. It will be considered by some as a blemish that she—a woman of fine spirituality—is made an artist's model, and some may even regret that such an episode mars the harmony of the drama. I cannot altogether see the force of this contention; it seems pure irrelevancy. But whatever may be thought of the fact, there is small room for complaint as to the handling of it. Ibsen treats it, as indeed he treats all things, with large insight, artistic restraint, and sympathy. He sees it steadily and whole, as from a great height, with perfect vision and an angelic dispassionateness, with the sight of one who may look on the sun with open eyes. Ibsen is different from the clever purveyor.

Maja fulfills a certain technical function in the play, apart from her individual character. Into the sustained tension she comes as a relief. Her airy freshness is as a breath of keen air. The sense of free, almost flamboyant, life, which is her chief note, counterbalances the austerity of Irene and the dullness of Rubek. Maja has practically the same effect on this play, as Hilda Wangel has on *The Master Builder*. But she does not capture our sympathy so much as Nora Helmer. She is not meant to capture it.

Rubek himself is the chief figure in this drama, and, strangely enough, the most conventional. Certainly, when contrasted with his Napoleonic predecessor, John Gabriel Borkman, he is a mere shadow. It must be borne in mind, however, that Borkman is alive, actively, energetically, restlessly alive, all through the play to the end, when he dies; whereas Arnold Rubek is dead, almost hopelessly dead, until the end, when he comes to life. Notwithstanding this, he is supremely interesting, not because of himself, but because of his dramatic significance. Ibsen's drama, as

I have said, is wholly independent of his characters. They may be bores, but the drama in which they live and move is invariably powerful. Not that Rubek is a bore by any means! He is infinitely more interesting in himself than Torvald Helmer or Tesman, both of whom possess certain strongly-marked characteristics. Arnold Rubek is, on the other hand, not intended to be a genius, as perhaps Eljert Lövborg is. Had he been a genius like Eljert he would have understood in a truer way the value of his life. But, as we are to suppose, the facts that he is devoted to his art and that he has attained to a degree of mastery in it—mastery of hand linked with limitation of thought—tell us that there may be lying dormant in him a capacity for greater life, which may be exercised when he, a dead man, shall have risen from among the dead.

The only character whom I have neglected is the inspector of the baths, and I hasten to do him tardy, but scant, justice. He is neither more nor less than the average inspector of baths. But he is that.

So much for the characterization, which is at all times profound and interesting. But apart from the characters in the play, there are some noteworthy points in the frequent and extensive side-issues of the line of thought. The most salient of these is what seems, at first sight, nothing more than an accidental scenic feature. I allude to the environment of the drama. One cannot but observe in Ibsen's later work a tendency to get out of closed rooms. Since *Hedda Gabler* this tendency is most marked. The last act of *The Master Builder* and the last act of *John Gabriel Borkman* take place in the open air. But in this play the three acts are *al fresco*. To give heed to such details as these in the drama may be deemed ultra-Boswellian fanaticism. As a matter of fact it is what is barely due to the work of a great artist. And this feature, which is so prominent, does not seem to me altogether without its significance.

Again, there has not been lacking in the last few social dramas a fine pity for men—a note nowhere audible in the uncompromising rigor of the early eighties. Thus in the conversion of Rubek's views as to the girl-figure in his masterpiece, "The Resurrection Day," there is involved an all-embracing philosophy a deep sympathy with the cross-purposes and contradictions of life, as they may be reconcilable with a hopeful awakening—when the manifold travail of our poor humanity may have a glorious issue. As to the drama itself, it is doubtful if any good purpose can be served by attempting to criticize it. Many things would tend to prove this. Henrik Ibsen is one of the world's great men before whom criticism can make but feeble show. Appreciation, hearkening is the only true criticism. Further, that species of criticism which calls itself dramatic criticism is a needless adjunct to his plays. When the art of a dramatist is perfect the critic is superfluous. Life is not to be criticized, but to be faced and lived. Again, if any plays demand a stage they are the plays of Ibsen. Not merely is this so because his plays have so much in common with the plays of other men that they were not written to cumber the shelves of a library, but because they are so packed with thought. At some chance expression the mind is tortured with some question, and in a flash, long reaches of life are opened up in vista, yet the vision is momentary unless we stay to ponder on it. It is just to prevent excessive pondering that Ibsen requires to be acted. Finally, it is foolish to expect that a problem which has occupied Ibsen for nearly three years will unroll smoothly before our eyes on a first or second reading. So it is better to leave the drama to plead for itself. But this at least is clear, that in this play Ibsen has given us nearly the very best of himself. The action is neither hindered by many complexities, as in *The Pillars of Society,* nor harrowing in its simplicity, as in *Ghosts.* We have whimsicality, bordering on extravagance, in the wild Ulfheim, and subtle humor in the sly contempt which Rubek and Maja entertain for each other. But Ibsen has striven to let the drama have perfectly free action. So he has not bestowed his wonted pains on the minor characters. In many of his plays these minor characters are matchless creations. Witness Jacob Engstrand, Tönnesen, and the demonic Molvik! But in this play the minor characters are not allowed to divert our attention.

On the whole, *When We Dead Awaken* may rank with the greatest of the author's work—if, indeed, it be not the greatest. It is described as the last of the series, which began with *A Doll's House*—a grand epilogue to its ten predecessors. Than these dramas, excellent alike in dramaturgic skill, characterization, and supreme interest, the long roll of drama, ancient or modern, has few things better to show.

—1900

The Day of the Rabblement

No MAN, said the Nolan, can be a lover of the true
or the good unless he abhors the multitude; and the
artist, though he may employ the crowd, is very careful to isolate himself. This radical principle of artistic economy applies specially to a time of crisis, and
today when the highest form of art has been just pre-
served by desperate sacrifices, it is strange to seé the
artist making terms with the rabblement. The Irish
Literary Theatre is the latest movement of protest
against the sterility and falsehood of the modern
stage. Half a century ago the note of protest was uttered in Norway, and since then in several countries
long and disheartening battles have been fought
against the hosts of prejudice and misinterpretation
and ridicule. What triumph there has been here and
there is due to stubborn conviction, and every movement that has set out heroically has achieved a little.
The Irish Literary Theatre gave out that it was the

champion of progress, and proclaimed war against commercialism and vulgarity. It had partly made good its word and was expelling the old devil, when after the first encounter it surrendered to the popular will. Now, your popular devil is more dangerous than your vulgar devil. Bulk and lungs count for something, and he can gild his speech aptly. He has prevailed once more, and the Irish Literary Theatre must now be considered the property of the rabblement of the most belated race in Europe.

It will be interesting to examine here. The official organ of the movement spoke of producing European masterpieces, but the matter went no further. Such a project was absolutely necessary. The censorship is powerless in Dublin, and the directors could have produced *Ghosts* or *The Dominion of Darkness* if they chose. Nothing can be done until the forces that dictate public judgement are calmly confronted. But, of course, the directors are shy of presenting Ibsen, Tolstoy or Hauptmann, where even *Countess Cathleen* is pronounced vicious and damnable. Even for a technical reason this project was necessary. A nation which never advanced so far as a miracle-play affords no literary model to the artist, and he must look abroad. Earnest dramatists of the second rank, Sudermann, Björnson, and Giacosa, can write very much better plays than the Irish Literary Theatre has staged. But, of course, the directors would not like to present such improper writers to the uncultivated, less to the cultivated, rabblement. Accordingly, the rabblement, placid and intensely moral, is enthroned in boxes and galleries amid a hum of approval—*la bestia Trionfante*—and those who think that Echegaray is "morbid," and titter coyly when Mélisande lets down her hair, are not sure but they are the trustees of every intellectual and poetic treasure.

Meanwhile, what of the artists? It is equally unsafe at present to say of Mr. Yeats that he has or has not genius. In aim and form *The Wind among the Reeds* is poetry of the highest order, and *The Adoration of the Magi* (a story which one of the great Russians might have written) shows what Mr. Yeats can do when he breaks with the half-gods. But an aesthete has a floating will, and Mr. Yeats's treacherous instinct of adaptability must be blamed for his recent association with a platform from which even self-respect should have urged him to refrain. Mr. Martyn and Mr. Moore are not writers of much originality. Mr. Martyn, disabled as he is by an incorrigible style, has none of the fierce, hysterical power of Strindberg, whom he suggests at times; and with him one is conscious of a lack of breadth and distinction which outweighs the nobility of certain passages. Mr. Moore, however, has wonderful mimetic ability, and some years ago his books might have entitled him to the place of honor among English novelists. But though *Vain Fortune* (perhaps one should add some of *Esther Waters*) is fine, original work, Mr. Moore is really struggling in the backwash of that tide which has advanced from Flaubert through Jakobsen to D'Annunzio: for two entire eras lie between *Madame Bovary* and *Il Fuoco*. It is plain from *Celibates* and the later novels that Mr. Moore is beginning to draw upon his literary account, and the quest of a new impulse may explain his recent startling conversion. Converts are in the movement now, and Mr. Moore and his island have been fitly admired. But however frankly Mr. Moore may misquote Pater and Turgénieff to defend himself, his new impulse has no kind of relation to the future of art.

In such circumstances it has become imperative to define the position. If an artist courts the favor of the multitude he cannot escape the contagion of its fetishism and deliberate self-deception, and if he joins in a popular movement he does so at his own risk. Therefore, the Irish Literary Theatre by its surrender to the trolls has cut itself adrift from the line of advancement. Until he has freed himself from the mean influences about him—sodden enthusiasm and clever insinuation and every flattering influence of vanity and low ambition—no man is an artist at all. But his true servitude is that he inherits a will broken by doubt and a soul that yields up all its hate to a caress; and the most seeming-independent are those who are the first to reassume their bonds. But Truth deals largely with us. Elsewhere there are men who are worthy to carry on the tradition of the o]d master who is dying in Christiania. He has already found his successor in the writer of *Michael Kramer,* and the third minister will not be wanting when his hour comes. Even now that hour may be standing by the door.

—1901

Catilina

THE FRENCH TRANSLATORS of this play have
included in their preface some extracts from Ibsen's
preface to the Dresden edition of 1875, and these extracts tell somewhat humorously the history of
Ibsen's early years. The play was written in 1848,
when Ibsen was twenty, a poor student working all
day in a druggist's shop, and studying during the
night as best he could. Sallust and Cicero, it seems,
awakened his interest in the character of Catiline, and
he set to work to write a tragedy, in part historical,
and in part political, a reflection of the Norway of his
day. The play was politely refused by the directors
of the Christiania Theatre and by all the publishers.
One of Ibsen's friends, however, published it at his
own expense, fully convinced that the play would at
once make the writer's name famous in the world. A
few copies were sold and, as Ibsen and his friend
were in need of money, they were glad to sell the re-

mainder to a pork-butcher. "For some days," Ibsen writes, "we did not lack the necessaries of life." This is a sufficiently instructive history, and it is well to remember it when reading a play which Ibsen publishes simply that his work may be complete. For the writer of *Catilina* is not the Ibsen of the social dramas, but, as the French translators joyfully proclaim, an ardent romantic exulting in disturbance and escaping from all formal laws under cover of an abundant rhetoric. This will not appear so strange when it is remembered that the young Goethe was somewhat given to alchemical researches, and as, to quote Goethe himself, the form in which a man goes into the shadows is the form in which he moves among his posterity, posterity will probably forget Ibsen the romantic as completely as it forgets Goethe and his athanor.

Yet, in some ways, this earlier manner suggests the later manner. In *Catilina* three figures are projected against the background of a restless and moribund society—Catiline, Aurelia, his wife, and Fulvia, a vestal virgin. Ibsen is known to the general public as a man who writes a play about three people—usually one man and two women—and even critics, while they assert their admiration for Ibsen's "unqualified objectivity," find that all his women are the same woman renamed successively Nora, Rebecca, Hilda, Irene—find, that is to say, that Ibsen has no power of objectivity at all. The critics, speaking in the name of the audience, whose idol is common sense, and whose torment is to be confronted with a clear work of art that reflects every obscurity like a mirror, have sometimes had the courage to say that they did not understand the system of three. They will be pleased to learn that some of the characters in *Catilina* are in as sorry a plight as themselves. Here is a passage in which Curius, a young relative of Catiline, professes his inability to understand Catiline's relations with Fulvia and Aurelia:

CURIUS: *Les aimerais-tu toutes deux à la fois ?*
   Vraiment je n'y comprends plus rien.
CATALINA: *En effet c'est singulier et je n'y*
   comprends rien moi-même.

But perhaps that he does not understand is part of the tragedy, and the play is certainly the struggle between Aurelia, who is happiness and the policy of non-interference, and Fulvia, who is at first the policy of interference and who, when she has escaped from the tomb to which her sin had brought her, becomes the figure of Catiline's destiny. Very little use is made in this play of alarms and battles, and one can see that the writer is not interested in the usual property of romanticism. Already he is losing the romantic temper when it should be at its fiercest in him, and, as youth commonly brooks no prevention, he is content to hurl himself upon the world and establish himself there defiantly until his true weapons are ready to his hand. One must not take too seriously the solution of the drama in favor of Aurelia, for by the time the last act is reached the characters have begun to mean nothing to themselves and in the acted play would be related to life only by the bodies of the performers. And here is the most striking difference between Ibsen's earlier manner and his later manner, between romantic work and classical work. The romantic temper, imperfect and impatient as it is, cannot express itself adequately unless it employs the monstrous or heroic. In *Catilina* the women are absolute types, and the end of such a play cannot but savor of dogma—a most proper thing in a priest but a most improper in a poet. Moreover, as the breaking-up of tradition, which is the work of the modern era, discountenances the absolute and as no writer can escape the spirit of his time, the writer of dramas must remember now more than ever a principle of all patient and perfect art which bids him express his fable in terms of his characters.

As a work of art *Catilina* has little merit, and yet one can see in it what the directors of the Christiania theatre and the publishers failed to see—an original and capable writer struggling with a form that is not his own. This manner continues, with occasional lapses into comedy, as far as *Peer Gynt,* in which, recognizing its own limitations and pushing lawlessness to its extreme limit, it achieves a masterpiece. After that it disappears and the second manner begins to take its place, advancing through play after play, uniting construction and speech and action more and more closely in a supple rhythm, until it achieves itself in *Hedda Gabler*. Very few recognize the astonishing courage of such work and it is characteristic of our age of transition to admire the later manner less than the earlier manner. For the imagination has the quality of a fluid, and it must be held firmly, lest it become vague, and delicately, that it may lose none of its magical powers. And Ibsen has united with his strong, ample, imaginative faculty a preoccupation with the things present to him. Perhaps in time even the professional critic, accepting the best of the social dramas for what they are—the most excellent examples of skill and intellectual self-possession—will make this union a truism of professional criticism. But meanwhile a young generation which has cast away belief and thrown precision after it, for which Balzac is a great intellect and every sampler who chooses to wander amid his own shapeless hells and heavens a Dante without the unfortunate prejudices of Dante, will be troubled by this preoccupation, and out of very conscience will denounce a method so calm, so ironical. These cries of hysteria are confused with many others—the voices of war and statecraft and religion—in the fermenting vat. But Boötes, we may be sure, thinks nothing of such cries, eager as ever at that ancient business of leading his hunting-dogs across the zenith "in their leash of sidereal fire."

—1903

Epilogue to Ibsen's Ghosts

Dear quick, whose conscience buried deep
The grim old grouser has been salving,
Permit one spectre more to peep.
I am the ghost of Captain Alving.

Silenced and smothered by my past
Like the lewd knight in dirty linen
I struggle forth to swell the cast
And air a long-suppressed opinion.

For muddling weddings into wakes
No fool could vie with Parson Manders.
I, though a dab at ducks and drakes,
Let gooseys serve or sauce their ganders.

My spouse bore me a blighted boy,
Our slavey pupped a bouncing bitch.
Paternity, thy name is joy
When the wise sire knows which is which.

Both swear I am that self-same man
By whom their infants were begotten.
Explain, fate, if you care and can
Why one is sound and one is rotten.

Olaf may plod his stony path
And live as chastely as Susanna
Yet pick up in some Turkish bath
His *quantum est* of *Pox Romana*.

While Haakon hikes up primrose way,
Spreeing and gleeing while he goes,
To smirk upon his latter day
Without a pimple on his nose.

I gave it up I am afraid
But if I loafed and found it fun
Remember how a coyclad maid
Knows how to take it out of one.

The more I dither on and drink
My midnight bowl of spirit punch
The firmlier I feel and think
Friend Manders came too oft to lunch.

Since scuttling ship Vikings like me
Reck not to whom the blame is laid,
YMCA, VD, TB
Or Harbormaster of Port-Said.

Blame all and none and take to task
The harlot's lure, the swain's desire.
Heal by all means but hardly ask
Did this man sin or did his sire.

The shack's ablaze. That canting scamp,
The carpenter, has dished the parson.
Now had they kept their powder damp
Like me there would have been no arson.

Nay more, were I not all I was,
Weak, wanton, waster out and out,
There would have been no world's applause
And damn all to write home about.

—1934

GREEN INTEGER
Pataphysics and Pedantry

Edited by Per Bregne
Douglas Messerli, *Publisher*

Essays, Manifestos, Statements, Speeches, Maxims,
Epistles, Diaristic Notes, Narratives, Natural Histories,
Poems, Plays, Performances, Ramblings, Revelations
and all such ephemera as may appear necessary
to bring society into a slight tremolo of confusion
and fright at least.

*

GREEN INTEGER BOOKS

History, or Messages from History Gertrude Stein [1997]
Notes on the Cinematographer Robert Bresson [1997]
The Critic As Artist Oscar Wilde [1997]
Tent Posts Henri Michaux [1997]
Eureka Edgar Allan Poe [1997]
An Interview Jean Renoir [1998]
Mirrors Marcel Cohen [1998]
The Effort to Fall Christopher Spranger [1998]
Radio Dialogs I Arno Schmidt [1999]
Travels Hans Christian Andersen [1999]
In the Mirror of the Eighth King Christopher Middleton [1999]
On Ibsen James Joyce [1999]

Laughter: An Essay on the Meaning of the Comic
Henri Bergson [1999]
Seven Visions Sergei Paradjanov [1998]
Ghost Image Hervé Guibert [1998]
Ballets Without Music, Without Dancers, Without Anything
Louis-Ferdinand Céline [1999]
On Overgrown Paths Knut Hamsun [1999]
Poems Sappho [1999]
Metropolis Antonio Porta [1999]
Hell Has No Limits José Donoso [1999]
Art *Poetic'* Olivier Cadiot [1999]
Fugitive Suns: Selected Poetry Andrée Chedid [1999]
Theoretical Objects Nick Piombino [1999]
Suicide Circus: Selected Poems Alexei Kruchenykh [1999]

BOOKS FORTHCOMING FROM GREEN INTEGER

Islands and Other Essays Jean Grenier
Operatics Michel Leiris
My Tired Father Gellu Naum
Manifestos/Manifest Vicente Huidobro
The Doll and *The Doll at Play* Hans Bellmer
[with poetry by Paul Éluard]
Water from a Bucket Charles Henri Ford
What Is Man? Mark Twain
American Notes Charles Dickens
To Do: A Book of Alphabets and Birthdays Gertrude Stein
Letters from Hanusse Joshua Haigh
[edited by Douglas Messerli]

Prefaces and Essays on Poetry William Wordsworth
Licorice Chronicles Ted Greenwald
The Complete Warhol Screenplays Ronald Tavel
Confessions of an English Opium-Eater Thomas De Quincey
The Renaissance Walter Pater
Venusburg Anthony Powell
Captain Nemo's Library Per Olav Enquist
Against Nature J. K. Huysmans
The Two-Fold Vibration Raymond Federman
Partial Portraits Henry James
Satyricon Petronius [translation ascribed to Oscar Wilde]